Overcoming the Co-Parenting Trap:

Essential Parenting Skills When a Child Resists a Parent

D1559148

John A. Moran, Ph.D., Tyler Sullivan, & Matthew Sullivan, Ph.D.

OVERCOMING BARRIERS INC.

Praise for *Overcoming the Co-Parenting Trap*

This book is a **must** read for parents when a child resists one of them. *Overcoming the Co-Parenting Trap* uses every-day scenarios and suggested responses to help parents help their child. No other book on the market is more to the point or more practical.

This is an informative and compassionate booklet, packed with useful skills for both the resisted parent and the favored parent. What I particularly love about it are all the sample statements that the authors provide for parents to make to each other and the child – especially during challenging moments. A very handy resource for parents experiencing the stress of a resistant child.

A timely and much needed practical guide to address the immensely complex and heartbreaking challenge of co-parenting after divorce when children resist or refuse contact with a parent. Using real-word examples, this books references the latest research and offers knowledgeable advice from leading experts to help parents and their children break the stalemate of hurt.

Debra K. Carter, Ph.D.
Author of *CoParenting After Divorce: A GPS for Healthy Kids*

Overcoming the Co-Parenting Trap is an excellent resource for parents trying to manage the conflicted divorce, especially when a child is resisting contact with one of his/her parents. With concise, direct, and professional guidance, the authors provide helpful skills for dealing with such resistance and moving parents and children forward, rather than keep them mired in the conflicts of the past. If you're stuck in a very high conflict divorce, with children who are resisting contact with you or the other parent, or you work with families engaged in such conflicts, this book is for you!

Philip M. Stahl, Ph.D., ABPP (Forensic)
Forensic Psychologist, Parenting After Divorce
Director, Forensic Programs, Steve Frankel Group, LLC

Overcoming the Co-Parenting Trap:

Essential Parenting Skills
When a Child Resists a Parent

Warning to Readers About the Limitations of this Guide

The authors recognize that there are tremendous complexities and immense risks for families navigating divorce with children. There are rarely simple solutions for co-parents stuck in conflict. Every family's situation is unique, and further, family dynamics are constantly changing.

The authors do not warrant that the information herein is complete or applicable to every situation and do not assume and hereby disclaim any liability to any person for any loss or damage caused by errors, inaccuracies, or omissions that may appear in this guide.

This guide should not be used as a substitute for therapeutic support from mental health professionals. It does not provide legal opinions nor legal advice and is not intended to serve as a substitute for the advice of licensed professionals. The authors are not engaged in rendering mental health, legal, or other professional services through this guide.

Users of this material are solely responsible for determining the applicability of any information contained in this guide to their situation.

Contents

Background, Family Camp, and Acknowledgments

THE ESSENTIAL SKILLS GUIDE grew from the authors' experiences working with families through Overcoming Barriers programs and private practice. Thankfully many people have collaborated in this work and contributed to this project.

The Overcoming Barriers Family Camp ("Camp") originated from the work of Peggie Ward, Ph.D., a clinical psychologist and leading expert in the field of parenting coordination, who attempted to reunify a resisted father with his son at Common Ground Center, a family camp in Vermont. The intervention was unsuccessful as the preferred parent did not follow court orders and the children refused to leave the car.

Dr. Ward began to develop a specialized intensive family camp model in collaboration with Common Ground Center, realizing the very complex and specific needs of families in which a child's resistance of a parent is deeply entrenched and out of proportion to the parenting skills deficits of the resisted parent. They assembled a team that included psychologists Matt Sullivan, Ph.D., and Robin Deutsch, Ph.D. and court personnel, judges and attorneys to develop a camp intervention model that would include all members of the restructured family system (parents, spouses, siblings, step-siblings). Camp is designed to deliver intensive treatment to high-conflict families in which a child is resisting or refusing a relationship with a parent.

For Camp, the entire restructured family is hosted at a sleep-away retreat where they are immersed in psycho-educational and skills building groups, family therapy sessions, and milieu therapy. Each morning there is a 3-hour group for the preferred parents, a 3-hour group for the resisted parents, and a 3-hour group for the children. In the afternoons, each family has individualized family sessions for the co-parents which may include the children. In the afternoons and evenings the staff organize fun activities for all Camp participants, which provide resisted parents and their children with a means of beginning to reconnect in a mutually enjoyable manner.

The overarching goals of the Overcoming Barriers Camp are to increase co-parenting communication and cooperation so that the parents can resolve ongoing family conflicts without litigation, and to increase positive connection between the child and the resisted parent. *Family members find that they get as much out of the program as they put in. The first steps, breaking the stalemate of the co-parenting trap, are often the hardest, and Camp provides families with extra support and encouragement during this critical juncture.*

Overcoming Barriers began in 2008. Camp's success is due in large part to contributions from the founders mentioned above; Common Ground Center Director Jim Mendell; Overcoming Barriers' Executive Director Carol Blane; Donna Feinberg, LICSW; Veronica Gadbois; Barbara Fidler, Ph.D.; and the many families who have participated.

Special acknowledgment is due to Shawn McCall, Ph.D. for his assistance in developing the Essential Skills guide, and to Transitioning Families in Sonoma, CA, for their innovative work with families and encouragement with this guide.

Introduction

WHEN A CHILD RESISTS A PARENT, both parents are faced with parenting challenges far outside the realm of everyday parenting. The resisted parent tries to save a relationship with a child who resists—sometimes rudely—affection, communication and connection. The preferred parent is dismayed as the child conveys unhappy, angry and anxious apprehensions about the resisted parent. Both parents confront extreme parenting challenges as they try to preserve their child's sense of family, love and security.

Beginning around 1985, the behavioral health community became broadly aware of the problem of children resisting their relationship with a parent following marital separation and divorce. Since then, the issue has been the subject of in-depth research and discussion, sometimes heated, about how a child's resistance to a parent may be related to family dynamics that include interpersonal family violence, child abuse, parental neglect, differences in parenting styles, children's temperaments, parental alienation, parenting skills deficiencies, personality disorders in parents, the attachment history of children, restrictive gatekeeping[1] by the preferred parent, the role of stepparents and extended family, and failed interventions by behavioral health counselors, litigation and the courts.

At Overcoming Barriers we believe that understanding and intervening in families in which a child is resisting a parent is a work in progress. Other than general agreement that in some families children resist a parent, and that their resistance might be justified, unjustified, or both, there is no single or simple explanation for why it happens or how to best respond. Furthermore, just as each family is unique, how they overcome their family relationship barriers will be unique. Still, there are commonalities in what families experience, how they get caught in the "family conflict trap," and how they work their way out of intractable conflict toward cooperation, negotiation, and solution-finding.

The essential parenting skills we present are based on the work and experience of the Overcoming Barriers Team and review of books and articles about parenting and divorce, parent-child contact problems, family therapy, negotiation and communication skills, and even international peace studies. In our experience, it is critical that we try to intervene on all the factors that contribute to a child resisting or rejecting a parent. The ideas and skills we present are from a wide array of sources and are not intended to endorse any one author or approach to the issues.

The essential parenting skills are examined in four areas: 1) the resisted parent and the resisting child; 2) the preferred parent and the resisting child; 3) co-parents and the co-

---

1. Austin, W., Pruett, M., Kirkpatrick, H., Flens, J. & Gould. J. (2013). Parental Gatekeeping and Child Custody/Child Access Evaluation: Part I: Conceptual Framework, Research and Application. *Family Court Review*, (51)3, 485-501.

parenting trap; and 4) working through anger, resentment and forgiveness.

Overcoming a child's resistance to a parent almost always is a complex and irksome process. The families asking to participate in an Overcoming Barriers program usually have had little success in reducing family conflict and restoring family relationships even with the assistance of the courts, attorneys and behavioral health professionals. Increasing each parent's skill in responding to the unique challenges of a resisting child appears to be a critical step for containing the conflict. The limited success of the courts and behavioral health professionals at resolving the parent-child relationship impasse seems to say that successful co-parenting is the best and possibly only solution to the problem. It is important to emphasize, however, that reducing the problem involves increasing the parent's ability to respond to the child *and* the parent's skillful interacting with their co-parent.

We hope that the material that follows helps parents to gain insight into the complex issues they face. Of equal or greater importance, **we hope parents will see the complex challenges their children and co-parents face.** Many concrete suggestions are presented and parents may find it useful to review relevant sections often for helpful reminders or to problem solve around ongoing parenting challenges.

Overview of the Problem

WHY DO CHILDREN RESIST A PARENT? Is it because the parent deserves it? Is it because the favored parent has undermined the child's relationship with the resisted parent, either consciously or unconsciously? Is it because the resisted parent did not establish a secure bond with the child during the marital years? Does the child prefer one parent because of differences in parenting styles, discipline or more material advantages in one home? Are there lifestyle elements that forge the child's alliance with one parent, such as shared religious beliefs, recreational interests or other gender-based preferences? Has a parent forged a relationship with an intimate other whom the child resists, or did the new relationship begin in a manner that the child finds morally objectionable? Or, has the child been caught in a series of disputes between the co-parents that lead him or her to side with one parent against the other? Each of these possibilities, and more, needs to be considered to understand and describe the factors that lead a child to resist a relationship with a parent. And, it may be that different factors contribute to the process in different ways at different points in time. It is complicated.

Here is a figure[2] that describes root causes that can result in a child resisting or rejecting a parent.

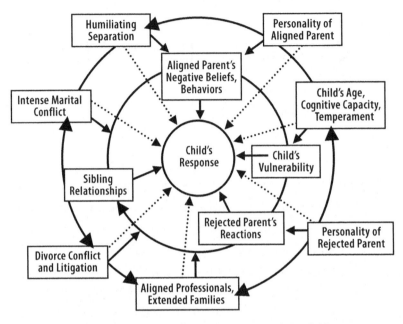

Figure 2. Background factors, intervening variables, and the child's response.

The outer circle in the figure represents *background* factors that might lead to a child resisting a parent. The second ring represents *personal factors* that influence the child's response.

Child Triangulated in Intense Marital Conflict
The child's risk for resisting a parent increases if the child was exposed to intense marital conflict prior to or following the separation, or if the child became a messenger between the parents, or a confidant and support for a parent in grieving

2. Kelly, J.B. & Johnston J.R. (2001). The Alienated Child: A Reformulation of Parental Alienation Syndrome. *Family Court Review*, (39)3, 249-266.

their loss of the marriage. It is not uncommon that prior to the separation, as the marital relationship deteriorated, one of the parents intensified their relationship with the children as a source of intimacy and affection, especially if the other parent was preoccupied outside the family.

A Deeply Humiliating Separation

A child is at increased risk for resisting a parent if a parent experiences the separation as deeply humiliating. For example, if the separation involved the discovery of an affair; emptying the house of possessions and the bank account of funds; discovery that the divorce had been planned for several months with the assistance of extended family; or, if the parent initiating the separation has a new relationship which challenges the family's existing notions of sexuality.

Intense Litigation

The risk of a child resisting a parent tends to increase if the family goes through an intense, continuing legal battle. Many children recognize that court proceedings are burdensome for the family, and they may view one parent as driving the court fight, which makes them angry at the parent they think is unnecessarily pushing the issue. Sometimes the child views one parent as having an unfair financial advantage and the child may sympathize with a parent they view as under too much financial stress.

New Partners

The risk of a child resisting a parent increases a lot if the child believes a new intimate relationship is responsible for the breakup of the family. Or, along the same line, if soon after the separation, a parent "re-partners" and the new partner makes a parenting misstep, such as using harsh criticism or discipline with the child or disparagement of the other parent.

Beliefs of the Parents

One theme is that the resisted parent is not safe—they have abused or neglected the child, or have been accused of abusing the child, and they are seen as likely to abuse the child in the future. Even though Camp families have been thoroughly screened for founded instances of abuse, concerns persist about the child's well-being when with the resisted parent. The preferred parent is stuck with apprehension and is torn between acting to protect the child and letting the child be exposed to what may be a risky situation when in the care of the resisted parent. Children can pick up, and even amplify, the belief that the resisted parent is not safe. The preferred parent may conclude that the children should not have family time with the resisted parent unless they feel comfortable doing so, or that the child needs time away from the resisted parent to heal. Or, based on the child getting emotionally upset when talking about their interactions with the resisted parent, the preferred parent may wonder if it is unhealthy for the children to spend time with the resisted parent.

The theme most commonly expressed by the resisted parent is that the child is resisting them because the other parent has alienated the child's affections and consciously and deliberately brainwashed the child into thinking the resisted parent is unsafe, scary or unable to parent the child effectively.

Usually by the time a family gets to Camp or another intensive intervention, arguments about the truth and evidence for such beliefs have been played out ad nauseam, that is, for so long that everyone is sick of it. The arguments have not clarified the source of the allegations of child maltreatment or confirmed the presence of parenting skills deficits; rather, the arguments have only led to further polarization, more deeply entrenched anger, more stubbornly held opposing beliefs, and, most importantly, a stronger alignment of the child with the preferred parent's beliefs.

One of our goals at Camp is to help parents appreciate that the issue is not an "either/or" situation; either that the resisted parent deserves it, or that the preferred parent alienated the child. Rather, it likely is a "both/and" situation, one in which complex forces are at work, unfortunate behavior has occurred, and unfortunate impacts have resulted. Arrival at a definitive conclusion about who did what to whom is not only unattainable, but unnecessary to getting the family unstuck from the conflict trap in which it is caught.

It should be noted that since the diagram on page 10 was published in 2001 there has been an explosion of Internet-based media on alienation. Much of the information available online is from parents with negative opinions about their co-parent; and, often from parents labeled as an alienating parent, or having been resisted by their children. The influence of Internet media can be added as another background cause resulting in a child resisting a parent. If parents and children look for information to support their negative views of the other parent, they are sure to find it on the web, further polarizing the family. Like all information on the Internet that may seem to resonate with one's experience, it is important to carefully evaluate its accuracy and usefulness.

Parenting the Child Who Resists Contact

IN THE BOOKS AND ARTICLES written about what makes for skillful parenting, overlapping ideas are encountered again and again; for example, skillful parents are warm and affectionate with their children, communicate with them effectively, use appropriate discipline techniques, and monitor and supervise their schoolwork, peer relationships and media exposure.

The onset of a child resisting a parent can be rapid, and the resisted parent may be unaware that the child has become resistant to them. The unsuspecting parent may become frustrated when regular parenting skills don't work. If, out of confusion and frustration, the resisted parent makes a parenting misstep, for example, by raising their voice or by using physical force or restraint, an interaction may occur that becomes hard proof to the child and other parent that resistance is justified.

Imagine that the resisting child is asked to evaluate the parenting of the preferred parent and the resisted parent on typical parenting tasks. The child assigns a grade for each parent using the traditional school grades, "A" equals excellent job; "B" equals good job; "C" equals average job; "D" equals needs improvement; and "F" equals failure. Here is what the report card of a resisting child might look like for the preferred parent (indicated with a "P") and the resisted parent (indicated with an "R").

My Mom (Preferred Parent)/ My Dad (Resisted Parent)	A	B	C	D	F
Offers love, caring, affection and encouragement	P+				R-
Communicates about personal and family events	P+				R-
Gives discipline consequences that are fair	P+				R--
Manages our home and my routines	P+			R	
Comforts me when I have difficult feelings	P++				R-
Makes it fun to be with him or her	P+				

When a child's attitude is so negative toward a parent, challenges to the parenting skills of the resisted parent are extreme, and rarely does a resisted parent have the special skills needed to respond to the child's anger without making the situation worse. In the next several sections we present general guidelines for the resisted parent for sharing affection, handling parent-child communication, using discipline, and participating in activities that generate positive parent-child interactions.

Skills for the Resisted Parent

Resisted Affection

Expressing affection to a resisting child can be tricky. A child may question a parent's good intentions or outright reject expressions of love and support. The parent doesn't want to stop expressing their affection but may need to be very reserved in expressing it in order to avoid more disaffection from the child.

When expressing love and support, the resisted parent should try to do it in a way that allows the child to receive the message without feeling the need to respond. Express to the child that you love them and care for them without making the child feel pressured to say anything. For example, say, "I love you no matter what," rather than, "Can I have a hug?" Remember, the important thing for the child to hear is that the parent loves them, is committed to them and will always be there for them no matter what (such as illustrated in the popular children's book *Runaway Bunny,* by Margaret Wise Brown).

When the resisted parent is stung with hurt, they may feel the urge to counter-reject the child by saying something like, "It's obvious you don't want to see me. I don't want to see you unless you do, so let me know when you want some time with me." Do not make this mistake. Instead, communicate to the child the message, "I will continue to love you regardless of what happens." Keep in mind that the child may not accept your calls, texts, holiday cards or gifts, but they are tracking if they arrived. Ironically, though the child may say they want no contact with you, later they may say that you not sending a birthday card or holiday gift is more proof that you do not really care and are not lovable.

Do not give up. This is a painful test of whether you love them unconditionally. Even when the child is resisting, they want love from both of their parents (although that wish may be unconscious at this point).

PARENTING TIPS:

• Do not insist on your child hugging or kissing you or your family members.

• Do not make long-winded or highly emotional statements about how much you love and miss your child.

• Show affection by sending cards and/or gifts for birthdays and holidays, even if they are returned.

• Show affection by showing up at extracurricular, school and sporting events (unless a court order prohibits attendance, or the parents have agreed to not attend activities at the same time).

• Show you care by considering your child's wish not to be around someone you are dating.

• Discourage extended family from contacting your child directly if he/she does not want it. Be sure to tell family members not to express their thoughts about the family conflict, who is to blame and how the child should be acting toward you and them.

Resistance to Parent-Child Communication

While working to improve the relationship, the resisted parent will repeatedly be challenged by the child to prove that they care; that they are safe to be with; and, that they are committed to skillful parenting over the long run. Be patient and long-suffering. If the child makes a hurtful statement such as, "If you loved me you would listen to what I am saying, that I don't want to spend time with you," a skillful response might be, "It makes me sad to hear you say that because I love you very much." Or if the child says, "You care more about your new girlfriend than about me and how I feel," you might say, "I understand that you feel that way, but you should know it's not true and I am going to keep doing what I can to prove it to you."

PARENTING TIPS:

• Work around highly emotional issues. If asked to talk directly about family relationships, a resisting child will typically shut down or argue, without giving thoughtful consideration to the ideas the parent wants the child to understand.

• Carefully orchestrate talks about sensitive issues. For example, ask the child if it is a good time to talk about a touchy subject and if the child says it is not, agree to talk later, or maybe ask for another time to schedule the conversation.

• Do not dismiss the child's negative attitudes and emotions by saying they should not be angry or afraid of you. Do not say that their feelings are caused by the preferred parent, or that their thoughts come from the preferred parent. The word "brainwashed" is a flashpoint for conflict.

Say something like, "I get it that you are really angry and disappointed in me. I want to respect those feelings and still try to make the best of our time together. I don't agree with much of what you are saying, but we probably can't talk through that at this point, so let's focus on making the best of things right now, and look forward to a time when we will be able to talk about some of these things and actually achieve a clearer understanding of what happened and what went wrong."

• Avoid arguing about what is true. Arguing about the facts of what happened, or what the facts mean, makes people feel discounted, defensive, self-righteous, resentful, and closed to the relationship. It may be possible to clarify simple facts about what happened in the past, like whether a vacation trip was in June or July, but the child's memories are colored by their interpretations that probably are not up for reconsideration.

• Avoid asking why your child is acting a certain way: Children may be incapable of verbalizing their feelings or hesitant because they feel intimidated.

• Children caught in the middle are very aware of the location of their parents and may act differently depending on who is present. A child's loyalty conflicts are heightened when both parents are present. Be aware of how the presence of siblings, especially older brothers and sisters, may affect a child's behavior and plan accordingly.

Resistance to Parental Discipline
When a child is resisting a parent, attempts to assert parental authority often are met with either active or passive resistance. For example, saying "You should do what I say because I am your

mother," is likely to be met with a nasty response whether it is verbally expressed or kept hidden. Discipline is to teach children how to get along in the world. Discipline is taking advantage of teaching moments to help the child understand how the world works, as much as it is about enforcing behavior standards and imposing behavioral consequences. With a resisting child, parents may do better to approach the child in a collaborative manner rather than as an authority figure. Some parents struggle with the idea that disciplining a child is a collaborative, or two-way process. After all, children should do what they are told to do. With a resisting child, however, the most important first step is to arrange enjoyable activities with the child that demonstrate that the parent-child relationship can work. It might be difficult to accept, but most resisted parents have very little success at enforcing behavior standards with children, and the punitive nature of discipline easily reinforces the child's belief that the resisted parent is mean, uncaring or doesn't listen.

PARENTING TIPS:

• Identify with the child potential points of friction before they happen. Plan activities with the child and get their preferences in advance, ideally when they are in a neutral mood.

• Talk with the child about what to do if either of you acts poorly. For example, "If you don't eat dinner with the family, you will not have access to your electronic devices." Or, "If I make a sarcastic comment or gesture about Mom, please point it out and I will apologize to you."

• Be ready for resistance: prepare your response and know your limits. In the example above, consider explaining the reason why eating dinner with the family is important. Focus on any positive consequences that go along with the desired behavior. Look out for the point when communication becomes unproductive, clarify the choices for the child and disengage.

• It is critical to avoid physical contact during a disciplinary event. For example, if the child grabs your hand to fight over possession of their cell phone, let them have it and address their aggression at another time.

• Inform the preferred parent of discipline events. The child may provide them a version that lacks important information.

Apologies by the Resisted Parent

Often children who are resisting a parent say that they need to receive an apology before they can begin to rebuild the relationship. Sometimes even a well-spoken apology will not work; for example, the child may say they could tell the parent really didn't mean what they said. Or, it may seem that the child wants the humiliation an apology can entail, more than a step toward reconciliation. As we discuss later in the section on forgiveness, the person receiving the apology has to be ready to receive it. Regardless, the resisted parent should be ready to skillfully respond to a child or to a co-parent's request or demand for an apology.

Perhaps making an apology should be approached as a process rather than a one-time event. That is, a parent could say, "I know you are owed an apology for things I have done in the past, both big and small. In fact, I am ready to apologize to you today, and I expect that I will need to or want to apologize to you again in the future, perhaps a bunch of times. I hope that you receive my apology with an open heart, and find your way to forgiveness for anything you think I have done that hurt you or our relationship."

PARENTING TIPS:

• Don't write the child a long letter or email explaining your perspective. Even if you do a beautiful and skillful job of it, and even if you offer an apology along with your explanation, it is unlikely to achieve your purposes. Why? Because inevitably some aspect of what you write will seem wrong to the child ("That's not what happened!"), or you will leave out parts they feel are the most important.[3]

• Use the "And Stance" – "You can be upset, and I can be upset too. You can feel you are right, and I can be right about some things too. I contributed to the problem, and you contributed too. We need to talk about both."

• Take responsibility for your contribution to the rift: "Looking back I can see…"

• Say what you are doing to ensure that past problems will not be repeated, "I keep in mind what you have said about my behavior and personality, and pay close atten-tion to when I act that way, or do not act that way. I have a couple of close friends I told about your concerns and asked them to say something to me if I am acting any-thing like that. I trust they are being honest with me and not just trying to make me feel better."

• If there is something you cannot apologize for, identify

---

3. Sheila Heen. Negotiating Conflicts, Part 1: Family Grudges. *The New York Times*. Published: December 11, 2013.

the impasse: "We have different memories about what happened. I know you feel I betrayed your trust in me. But we don't see eye-to-eye on what happened (for example, allegations of sexual mistreatment, domestic violence, abusive discipline, etc.). It seems we need to put that aside for now with the hope that in the future we will be able to talk about it."

•   Talk about what you want in the future: "I would like to spend time with you enjoying family activities, having fun without worrying about whether our past problems are going to keep popping up."

•   Close by validating their emotions: "I know that you have gut-wrenching feelings about how difficult our relationship has become; so do I. I appreciate that because the feelings are so deep and strong it will take a lot for us to feel comfortable with one another. I hope that my apology is a first step in that direction."

#1 Goal For the Resisted Parent: Positive Interactions with the Child

It is unusual for behavioral health professionals to say that talking about a problem can be the problem, but when a child is harboring anger and resentment, rather than trying to talk the child through their negative emotions, it is more important for them to have time with you that is pleasant and shows that you are committed to helping them make the best of the situation, even if it can't be improved quickly or easily.

Communication is a huge component of any activity, so we begin with some discussion of communication methods that will be useful in planning activities and during the activities themselves. As suggested earlier, collaborate with the child that you two share a horrific problem and have to work together to find a way to restore your relationship.

Here is a scenario: a child is playing ball in the house, and the parent is worried something may get broken. The parent-as-authority option would be: "Don't play with the ball in the house." A collaborative option would be: "I know that playing ball in the house is fun, but I'm worried about that vase on the counter. How about moving your game outside?" Rather than utilizing the parent's authority, the parent is appealing to the laws of physics and the child's judgment. It's the same message, but it gives the child agency and independence. At this point, what is the advantage of being authoritarian?

In making plans with a child, the resisted parent should minimize the use of questions and statements, which require an affirmative response. Instead of asking "Do you want spaghetti for dinner?" a parent expecting to encounter resistance might say "Unless you want something different, I am going to make spaghetti for dinner."

The resisted parent and the resisting child usually have very different ideas about how to work on restoring their communication. The resisted parent feels a pressing need to return to normal parent-child chit-chat. The child usually feels that the resisted parent wants too much too soon, and consequently, that the resisted parent is not listening to them or respecting their feelings. The resisted parent needs to acknowledge the child's attitude and acknowledge the child's efforts by saying something like, "I know that you don't feel that you want to talk to me. It may feel like opening-up to communicating with me is scary. Or maybe the anger you have toward me makes you want to pull back. How about if we agree that we will try to talk when we are together, and that you will tell me if I say something that doesn't work for you. Maybe you can even give me examples of how I could have said it better. I'd like to be able to give you feedback too."

Children may be rude or intentionally try to hurt a resisted parent's feelings. Ignoring such communication will set a bad precedent over time, while showing emotion or making a big deal of such behavior may be feeding into their intended purpose of being rude or hurtful. Resisted parents may find that addressing such comments lightly, while not digressing or dwelling on the behavior, will make the best of a challenging situation and avoid derailing a parent's time with the kids. For example, if a child says "Your hair is especially ugly today," a parent might respond "That's not a nice thing to say to someone who just spent all morning getting pretty/handsome for you! I guess I should have worn a hat."

PARENTING TIPS

• During planned activities, avoid discussion of challenging or emotional issues. Children under the stress of visiting with a resisted parent typically shut down or argue if asked to talk about family problems, and do not give thoughtful consideration to the ideas the parent wants them to understand. Older children may avoid discussing deep issues because they don't want the resisted parent to get the impression they are comfortable with them in any way, let alone talking about personal matters.

• During activities, do not ask the child why they are acting a certain way. He or she may resent being asked to talk about something they don't want to, they may be incapable of getting their feelings into words, or they may feel that verbalizing their thoughts and feelings may get them into trouble.

• While humor can be an effective way to redirect an uncomfortable situation or create a positive atmosphere, too much joking or a poorly timed joke can hurt the children's feelings or take away from an important message or conversation.

• Manage your own expectations about what a positive connection looks like. Expect to make progress in baby steps; learn to see the small signs of an improving relationship and build on those incremental improvements.

Activity Planning

Planning and structuring positive activities for a child and the resisted parent is challenging. The good news is that parents can prepare, put a lot of thought into the activities, and have a number of options available. If the activities don't work, go back to the drawing board.

Depending on the developmental level of the children, parents may be able to anticipate the attitudes, moods, interests and complaints of the children. Resisted parents might anticipate that children won't be appreciative or acknowledge they had a good time, particularly in front of (or later expressed to) the preferred parent or mental health professionals who might be involved. However, the child may choose the same activity in the future if given the choice, which is more reliable information than the child's verbal disapproval.

Activities that worked well in the past may not work during this breaking-the-ice period. In some cases, activities that were staples and always a hit in the past will fail miserably. Remember that play is a skill that can be developed over time, and parents may benefit from working at it on their own. Keep at it and do your best to pick the best activities for the situation. In choosing activities, particular attention should be given to each activity's requirements for the following:

1. verbal interaction between participants,
2. spatial proximity of participants,
3. physical interaction between participants,
4. visual, face-to-face contact,
5. number of participants,
6. skills required/ease of learning skills,
7. whether there is a winner, and therefore a loser,
8. whether the parent will be dominant, and if so, will the parent play down to the child's level?
9. whether the child has experience that can be applied to the activity, and if so, can the child teach the parent?
10. how long one can expect to continue the activity before it fizzles,
11. whether there is a risk for injury, and if so, is it worth the risk or can the risk be mitigated?

An example of a relatively neutral, safe, and positive activity for a resisted parent and a preteen or teenager is an art activity at a public arts and crafts studio. Both parent and child are usually beginners, creating a level playing field. It is a unique activity and likely to be memorable, especially if there is a tangible piece of art created. An instructor keeps things moving and helps to keep the mood light. There is room for lots of interaction, including opportunities for the parent to praise the child in a natural manner. However, the activity does not require lots of interaction; participants can focus on their individual art/ craft. There are do-it-yourself ceramic studios that provide a nice atmosphere and quality materials on a drop-in basis (for example see www.colormemine.com).

To take the pressure off children when it comes to choosing activities, provide a few diverse and open-ended options. The child should get the message that the important thing for the parent is to spend time with the child, irrespective of the activity. The choices a parent presents can help to relay this message. Here are a few scenarios of activity choices:

1. One resisted mother said to her 14-year-old son, "For our time next week, I was thinking we could go to the bookstore and look at SAT preparation books, then go to the mall and pick out some clothes for school, then maybe get some food or see a movie."

Comment: There is not very much room for choice here. The limited options seem to be driven by the parent's interests.

2. One resisted father said to his 10-year-old son, "For our visit next week, we can go to the batting cages because I know you love baseball. Then we can get some food and watch the game at my house."

Comment: There is not much choice or room for the child to control the visit. The father has linked the activity to himself by saying "I know you love baseball." The child may feel more compelled to reject the activity because of this link to his father, and because he doesn't want to imply that father knows what he likes.

3. One resisted mother said to her 12-year-old daughter: "For our time next week, I have a couple ideas, but thought you might have some ideas too. The county fair is going on downtown, and we could go on some rides and eat hamburgers. Or, we could go to the park and see if we can join a soccer game. Or, I am open to something else if you have something in mind."

Comment: Here the parent made it clear that she is open to suggestions. One option she presented required a lot of interaction, others, less so. Option two is physical; option one is less physical. Additionally, the third option is the child's choice.

Transparency and dialogue with children in activity planning can be very powerful if they promote collective problem solving or if the children are able to see that their parents are working to meet their needs. (It should go without saying that it is also extremely useful to get input from the expected participants when attempting to design a positive, interactive activity.) Teenagers, in particular, will benefit from having options and being supported in making choices, even with small things. It is a normal part of development for teenagers to want some independence and control over their lives, and learning to make smart choices and deal with the consequences is an important skill for all children to develop.

In some cases this dialogue may create friction or provide opportunities for children to sabotage activities. A consistent and skillful response to such a situation might include saying "I have been trying to get your input and even give you control over what we do with our time together, but I am not sure it is helping to make our time more positive. What do you think?" This neutral feedback may help the child to see the resisted parent's efforts and simultaneously hold the child accountable for their contribution (or lack of contribution) to the activities shared with the resisted parent.

Another response might be for a resisted parent to present options but also establish the boundary for when this option will have run its course. The child will have to adjust their behavior if they want to continue the activity. For example: "We have been playing chess a lot for the last few months. I don't think that we have finished a match yet, and the last two games ended with both of us in a bad mood. I am thinking that if this pattern continues we should try a game that takes less time or a game that is more active and see if we can end in a better mood."

Children may need time and space to work through these interactions and weigh their decisions. They may test limits to see if there will be follow through, or if the parent will give up or lose their patience. You will notice that the language above allows for flexibility so that the expectations are set, but still contingent on further discussion. This helps avoid getting stuck either having to follow through with an unhelpful, previously set limit, or not following through on that limit.

Activity planning is a major challenge for resisted parents and there is no guarantee that these planning strategies will help things to improve. Some resisted parents may decide it makes the most sense to plan activities unilaterally to avoid conflict, at least for some amount of time. Outsourcing activity planning to a professional or third party may be another way to avoid conflict if the dynamics of choosing an activity are so intolerable and counter-productive.

PARENTING TIPS:
- If the child seems overly stressed, consider giving them the option of ending early while making it clear that you

would like to continue the visit and that visits will not always end early. For example, the parent might say, "We seem to be struggling with one another today. Maybe we should wrap-up and take time to digest the day. I want to find ways of spending time with you that you enjoy. We can try something different next time." This sends a clear message that the child's comfort is primary in the parent's consciousness and that the parent is flexible, while making it clear that the parent wants to spend as much time as possible with the child. A parent might add "spending time with you is the best part of my week."

- Know which activities are your "go to" activities. Be careful, however, because overuse will make them grow stale. You may start visits with a "go to" activity before switching to another activity. That way, the parenting time gets off to a positive start, while avoiding complaints about boredom, or that the visits always "involve the same dumb activities. You always do the same things."

- If an activity isn't going well, it is okay to change the activity or take a break. A parent might suggest a break by saying, "Should we take a break and eat a snack? When we come back we can pick up where we left off or move on to something else afterwards."

- Planning activities collaboratively with the child is great practice for collaborating on other family issues, like with your co-parent. Take note of strategies that work; it might be helpful to report them to your co-parent as a model for your co-parenting relationship.

- Sibling participation in activities should be considered thoughtfully. Take time and make every effort to spend quality time with each child. It may be tempting to focus on the older children, especially if younger siblings follow their lead. Siblings may compete for attention, or in the case of resistance, may compete for who can be the rudest. When this occurs, having separate visits for each child is strongly encouraged.

• Consider how adding or subtracting people from activities will change the dynamics. Is it helpful to have friends join in? Cousins? If so, remember to be tactful and not to surprise children.

• Going out to dinner is a standard activity that presents many challenges. Interactions will be physically close over an extended period of time with ample opportunities for awkwardness. Consider the venue carefully and find the right seats, maybe even go on a restaurant tour. Can you sit with plenty of space or facing out (not face-to-face)? Are there televisions or other distractions? Can you play board games, read magazines together, or doodle? Is it a quiet place or bustling with waiters and other people? Will the children like the menu? Can you go for a walk nearby for dessert?

Skill-Building Challenges for Resisted Parents

Children who resist a parent can be rude, stubborn, disrespectful, defiant, provocative and threatening. Resisted parents will be put in difficult situations with high stakes, plenty of pressure and emotions running high. Advanced training and rehearsal for responding to extreme challenges by a resisting child is a must-do. When police officers, pilots, soldiers and emergency responders are interviewed by the media after a critical incident, they often say that training for the catastrophe was the key to their effectiveness; that their training took over, there wasn't time to analyze the situation and plan a good response.

Listed here are some examples of difficult parenting scenarios a resisted parent might confront. Think about how you would respond, then consider how alternative approaches might play out for your connection with your child, both in the immediate and longer terms. Discuss these challenges and the merits of various responses with people in your support network.

- Your child says that you don't pay Dad what he is owed, even though you do.

- Your child says, "You say that you've changed, but I don't feel like you've changed."

- You praise your child, tell him he is smart and funny. He responds, "You're so fake."

- Your child starts to call you by your first name rather than "Dad" or "Mom."

- You think that Mom buys the children's love by not having structure, by trying to be a friend rather than a parent. You tell the kids that at your house they have to obey your rules, and they say, "That's why I'd rather live with Mom. Your rules are stupid."

- You are talking to your child, but she is looking past you, glancing at her phone and obviously not paying attention. You ask her to repeat what you said, but she cannot.

- Your child says something mean to a sibling who is nice to you.

- You remind your child of the vacations and other special

activities you have done together, yet he acts like it doesn't matter.

- Your child says that you don't care about his feelings or you wouldn't take Mom back to court.

- Your child is nice to you only when she wants you to give her money.

- The child texts the preferred parent multiple times throughout the day, which you feel interferes with your parenting time.

- The child is in a good mood until they have their nightly telephone call with Mom; then they become sullen and withdraw.

- Your child keeps bringing up an isolated incident from the past when you lost your cool and said something mean about Dad.

- One of your children enjoys a week-on/week-off schedule. An older sibling comes over only when the court order requires and is open about their wish not to come over at all. What do you say if the older child becomes critical of the schedule in front of the younger child?

- Your child defiantly asks, "Why do I have to do that (chore)?" You say, "Because we are a family and we each pitch in." The child says, "I don't want to be part of this family."

- Your child says that Mom's boyfriend said you are not a good father.

- You ask your child to pray with you before bedtime, and she prays that she doesn't have to sleep at your house anymore.

- You shop with the child's food preferences in mind, and he tells the co-parent that you don't have nutritious food around the house.

- You discover that your child has been posting on Facebook vicious and untrue statements about you.

- Your child says that he is afraid to spend time with you although he has no basis for such fear. Do you insist he comes over? How do you address his concern?

- In front of her friend, your daughter says, "You are a pervert."

- You give your children presents and they say, "You're bribing us!"

Skills for the Preferred Parent

Responding to a Child's Complains about the Other Parent[4]
Taking your child's complaint onto your own shoulders and doing battle can be toxic: 1) it communicates that the child may be unable to handle the problem and that adults should step in; 2) it offers you an opening to react based on historical resentments that have nothing to do with your child; 3) doing battle for your child will only sustain rather than resolve his/her relationship problems with the other parent, and 4) your efforts to intervene may be seen by others, including the Court, as undermining and alienating. The ears of overprotective or fearful parents get very, very big whenever the kids say anything negative about their other parent. This does not escape a child's notice; they learn that you listen more intently than usual if they report something negative about the co-parent. Remember: 1) children exaggerate; 2) children elaborate on details; 3) children leave out important details; and, 4) children sometimes lie.

In families when a child resists a parent, usually both parents worry that their co-parent is making negative, critical, unjustified, and untrue statements about them to the child, reading court documents to the child, or allowing the child to

---

4. Jeffrey P. Wittmann, Ph.D. (2001). *Custody Chaos, Personal Peace: Sharing Custody with an Ex Who Drives You Crazy.* New York: Perigee Books.

hear them talk critically to family members or friends. It can be helpful for the parents to adopt a written agreement about the expression of criticism within the family. The written agreement can be read to the child either when the co-parents are together or each in their own homes.

Sample Co-parenting Agreement to be Read to the Children when They Complain About Their Co-Parent

It is our divorce. You should not have to feel responsible for it, hear about it, or provide emotional support for us as we go through it. You should not have to ensure that either of us is behaving properly about it.

We want your childhood to be safe, secure and devoted to the problems children have, not to our adult problems.

Here are our rules:

- Neither parent is allowed to make critical statements about the other.

- If you hear us make a critical statement about one another, please point out that we are breaking the rule, and you may tell the other parent what you heard said, if you wish.

- You are not allowed to read court documents, read our text messages or emails to one another, or overhear our conversations with other adults about divorce-related matters. It is your responsibility and ours to ensure that you are not exposed to such matters.

- If one of us seems angry or upset about the divorce, please don't ask us to talk about it or even listen to us if we speak out loud our distress; instead, give us time and space. We are competent adults and can take care of our own business although sometimes we need a time-out to settle our emotions.

- If you have a complaint about either of us, talk to us directly rather than your other parent. Everyone has to learn to address relationship problems. We know it can be tough for a kid to be direct with a parent; we will help you along if you start the talk. But going forward, if you complain to me about Mom/Dad, I will listen politely, and ask you to bring the issue to Mom/Dad; I won't jump in for you.

- However, if you tell one of us that you have an issue with your other parent and are not comfortable to talk to your other parent directly, we can all meet together, and I will do my best to help you talk about your issue without talking for you. [Note: if the child has a counselor, the parent should direct the child to share their concerns and issues with the counselor.]

When a Child Refuses Parenting Time

Children can be adamant that they do not want to be with the resisted parent, and argue dramatically about why they should not have to go. The preferred parent is faced with having to insist that the children participate, even as the resisted parent seems ready to pounce if their parenting time does not occur. And the child may return home in a bad mood or with complaints. The preferred parent is caught between the tiger and the cliff, and may be unsure about what to do, or even if the parenting plan should be followed.

There are many reasons a child should be required to address and overcome their resistance to a parent — some are obvious and some are counterintuitive. When a child loses a relationship with a parent, they lose 50% of their genetic and cultural identity. Not all children who resist or refuse contact with a parent suffer long-term psychological consequences, but many do. Behavioral health researchers[5] have found that children caught in a prolonged dispute about parenting time may develop *internalizing disorders* such as social withdrawal, stress-related physical health complaints, depression or anxiety; or, *externalizing disorders* such as aggressive or antisocial behaviors and hyperactive symptoms.

If a parent had an accident and died, everyone would express profound sympathy for the impact on the child. If a child loses a relationship with a parent and extended family because the co-parents cannot get past their own feelings to find a way to preserve the family, the child gets support, but may also get the message that they are a victim, entitled to anger and resentment.

Sometimes a preferred parent hopes that over time the child will experience a spontaneous reconciliation of their issues with the resisted parent; that time will heal the wounds, or the child will grow out of it. That sometimes happens, but when a child has limited contact with that parent, it is less likely.

Not intervening to resolve the resistance creates various risks. The child may be left with painful memories of their parents' dispute, and with questions about how each parent responded to the family's crisis. That is, what kind of a role model was each of the parents for how to address and resolve highly stressful relationship challenges? In the absence of a clear message from the preferred parent, children will make assumptions or create their own beliefs based on what information they have.

---

5. See for example, Fidler, B.J., Bala N.& Saini, M.A. (2013). *Children Who Resist Postseparation Parental Contact; a Differential Approach for Legal and Mental Health Professionals*, (2013). New York: Oxford University Press.

The expression of even mild ambivalence by the preferred parent can put kids in the middle of their parents' conflict by default. Co-parents in conflict are challenged to compartmentalize their negative feelings toward one another so that the only message the child gets is to appreciate having two committed parents. A danger for the parents is that they will transmit, directly or indirectly, their negative thoughts and feelings toward the co-parent, and the children will listen closely to those communications. If the parent communicates ambivalence, the children may get the impression they have the choice to connect or not to connect. If a parent communicates ambivalence, children may feel pressure to refuse as a way of showing solidarity with the preferred parent's experience, to avoid hurting the feelings of the preferred parent, or simply because it is easier to avoid the complexity of the situation. The child may wonder if by choosing to spend time with the resisted parent, the family and family court professionals will think they *enjoy* it, want to increase contact, or change custody. Many children express relief when someone else takes over parent-child contact decisions because it takes the burden of having to balance their parents' needs off their shoulders.

The thoughts expressed by children to explain why they are resisting a parent typically reflect immature and lower levels of critical thinking skills. Their thoughts tend to be one-sided negative portrayals of the resisted parent; they often offer superficial reasons for their attitudes; they refuse to consider other reasonable points of view; or, to reflect on how their thinking might be viewed as angry, stubborn, and vindictive. For parents, addressing the relationship impasse may be extremely difficult, but the alternative is to reinforce the notion that emotional excesses are tolerable and form a good enough basis for making important life decisions. Children who resist a parent believe it is okay for them to be disobedient, defiant and to withdraw from interpersonal problems rather than being reasonable, persistent, and resourceful. Later in life they may experience shame, guilt, and regret from having resisted their parent.

For a child resisting a parent, the risk of impact on their future ability to form intimate attachments is significant. Three decades of research have demonstrated that forming intimate attachments is key to well-being. The child's attachment with the preferred parent insulates them from the massive disruption they would experience if they had no secure primary attachments, but loss of relationship with a parent can negatively impact the child's long-term ability to successfully negotiate the challenges of romance and having a family.

Recently, behavioral health researchers have been documenting the impact of dysfunctional family relationships on the child's risk for not only mental health disorders, but also major chronic diseases and early mortality.[6] For example[7], researchers examined data from Harvard undergraduate men in the early 1950's from divorced families and whether their relationship with each parent was positive or negative. Thirty-five years later, the researchers examined available medical records of the research subjects and found that of the men who

---

6. Repetti, R.L., Taylor, S.E., & Seeman, T.E. (2002). Risky families: Family social environments and the mental and physical health of offspring. *Psychological Bulletin*, 128, 330-366.

7. Cited in Fabricius, W.V., Sokol, K.R., Diaz, P. & Braver, S. (2012). Parenting Time, Parent Conflict, Parent-Child Relationships, and Children's Physical Health. In *Parenting Plan Evaluations: Applied Research for the Family Court.* Kuehnle, K. & Drozd, L. (Eds.), New York: Oxford University Press.

described a negative relationship with either their mother or their father, 85% to 91% had developed a cardiovascular disease, duodenal ulcer and/or alcoholism, compared to only 45% to 50% of the men who described positive relationships with both parents. It should be emphasized that the results of one study do not lead to a strongly supported conclusion, but the study seems to confirm the suspicion that exposing children to a series of emotionally distressing relationship encounters can impact their organs, brain, and immune system.

The bottom line is that each family member is obligated to comply with the court-ordered parenting plan. But there are several scenarios in which preferred parents may feel ambivalent about the wisdom of requiring the children to follow the parenting time plan, and because of their ambivalence, they may not be motivated enough to succeed in getting the children to go. Below we describe several scenarios that can undermine the preferred parent's motivation to ensure that children follow the court-ordered parenting time plan.

The Children Should Have a Voice Scenario

There is no dispute that children's thoughts, feelings, and wishes should be considered, carefully. The importance of the children's wishes varies with their age and maturity. It is not unusual for a preferred parent to ask "At what age can children decide?" Or to say, "I support the children's relationship with the co-parent if that is what they want." Perhaps in the past, the preferred parent honored the children's wishes to avoid or minimize contact with the resisted parent, but now the court ordered a new parenting time schedule. The preferred parent may be challenged to regain control of a situation that the children have come to believe they ought to be able to control.

The Better Safe Than Sorry Scenario

Perhaps the child has made an allegation of abuse against the co-parent, step-parent, or a step-child living with the co-parent, and the preferred parent believes there is a credible basis to believe the allegation. The preferred parent may support the child's resistance to scheduled parenting time fearing that if they send the child, abuse may occur. They may worry that they will be held responsible by child protective services for sending the child into a situation in which a credible threat of abuse existed, and risk the potential loss of their parental rights.

The Stress on the Child is Excessive

As the child approaches parenting time they are resisting, they may complain of stress-related symptoms such as stomach aches, headaches, or even thoughts of harming themselves. The preferred parent may wonder if the stress on the child poses a risk of harm that outweighs the value of parenting time with the resisted parent.

Children Deserve a Safe and Carefree Childhood

If the divorce litigation has been grueling, and the children were subjected to evaluations and unsuccessful behavioral health interventions, a preferred parent may conclude their children deserve a break or time-out from the turmoil that surrounds their relationship with the resisted parent. The preferred parent may feel that their responsibility is to provide the children a few years of "normal" childhood experience, even if that means their relationship with the co-parent has to be put on hold.

The Co-parent(s) Doesn't Know How to Parent the Child

It is commonly understood that following divorce, most co-parenting relationships are fragile. The hurt of divorce tends to smolder for several years, then linger as an enduring sadness. Against this emotional background, a parent may think that although the powerful impact of the divorce has changed them, it has not had a significant impact on the co-parent; that the co-parent continues to have critical parenting or personality deficits they observed during the marriage. The preferred parent may feel obligated to protect the children against the creeping negative effect of this alleged parenting skills and personality disorder.

It Was Going OK until Stepparent Got Involved

Blending families is more difficult than most parents anticipate. Often, the introduction of a new partner or a stepparent makes the family dynamics either significantly better or significantly more difficult. If the latter, the preferred parent may feel renewed confusion about the wellbeing of the children when in the care of the other parent.

Preferred Parent's Lack of Control

Perhaps the preferred parent is strongly motivated to make the child have contact with the resisted parent, but the preferred parent believes they have lost control of the child's behavior. The preferred parent allowing children to control parenting time decisions is worrisome. Families are organized with a hierarchy of authority — the parents manage the children. When co-parenting fails, other family members, clergy, counselors or the law (in the form of child protective services, the police, court-appointed professionals, attorneys and the courts) may be brought in to help with, or even take over, management of the children. If the aligned parent does not have the ability to implement the parenting plan, the court may take action to assure that the child is properly managed by requiring the aligned parent to participate in individual counseling, ordering that the family participate in an intensive intervention such as the Overcoming Barriers Camp, or even order that the resisted parent be given primary responsibility for the children, including where they live.

Responding to the Child's Refusal

Parents should approach their child refusing parenting time as they would approach the child refusing to attend other critical events. When the child resists, how does the parent get them to attend doctor's appointments, school, or visits with extended family? Part of the solution must include communicating to the child that it is essential to have family time with the resisted parent. It is relatively easy to explain why a medical appointment is necessary, but the preferred parent may have to work in counseling to clarify the value of the co-parent in the child's life, and what they can say to express meaningful support for the resisted parent's efforts to unify with the child.

The parents have to work together to overcome the child's resistance. The argument that the cause of the child's resistance is about deficits in the co-parent is short-sighted; the problem is rooted in years of marital disharmony and co-parenting disagreements. The preferred parent is part of the cause-effect chain; it is not accurate to claim that they are neutral to what is going on between the child and the resisted parent. Rather, they must actively help the resisted parent repair the relationship with the child. It is a co-parenting issue just like attending any other important event or place, such as school.

The preferred parent has a delicate role in helping the child to overcome resistance. They have to respect and acknowledge the child's feelings while challenging the child's point of view. The child may only want support messages such as, "It's sad that you have such a troubled relationship with Mom," and may feel that the preferred parent is disloyal to them if they get messages such as, "I know it is hard, I know you feel upset, but I expect you to tackle this problem head-on, it's that important." Or, if they get a message such as, "I know you don't like to hear it, but there are a lot of different ways to understand what is going on, and we owe it to ourselves and your Mom to be as careful and open to this situation as we can be." The preferred parent has to let the child know that they view the child's problems with the other parent as a matter of supreme importance, and that they are committed to helping the child work on it with everyone that needs to be involved, be that themself, the other parent or stepparent, siblings, or a counselor.

A preferred parent helping a child past their resistance to their other parent means helping the child to see that while the current situation is challenging, awkward, emotional and confusing, both parents love them and things will get better with time.

An often used, and often ineffective, intervention when a child refuses court-ordered parenting time, is to send the child to counseling alone or just with the resisted parent. This intervention reinforces the mistaken idea that the issue is a parent-child problem rather than a family systems problem. This approach makes the child significantly responsible for repairing a problem rooted in co-parenting conflict. The preferred parent has more leverage than the resisted parent to convince the child that a new approach to the family's chronic conflict is needed. Even with vigorous support from the preferred parent, the resisted parent will be fully challenged to develop and use better parenting skills to restore their relationship with the resisting child.

There are no quick or easy fixes to the problem of a child refusing contact with the resisted parent. Allowing the child to stay home may seem to be the easiest path. However, it is our experience that permitting children to miss their time with the resisted parent is a slippery slope. Missed contacts leave the resisted parent with little recourse other than to blame the preferred parent.

PARENTING TIPS:

• The sooner and more clearly you establish that contact with the resisted parent is not negotiable, the sooner you can move past debating the point and begin helping the children to problem solve around how to make their interactions with the other parent more positive. This limit setting may require consequences for missing visits such as loss of use of cell phones, grounding, loss of television or favorite toys. If this doesn't work, consider attending counseling with the child to clarify that you are listening closely to them and want to respect their wishes, but family time with the resisted parent is critical.

• Problem solving relationship issues is a skill we all need. Help the child to identify the challenges precisely. For example, "being at Mom's house is hard because there is no quiet place to do my homework and she always makes me eat gross food," rather than "I hate these visits, Mom is so annoying."

• Create positive incentives to help the child work through challenges related to parenting time with the resisted parent. Reminding them of the behavior to be re-

warded will help build the child's self-awareness and provide extra opportunities for parents to do the important
work of teaching positive coping skills. Younger children
benefit from more immediate and structured feedback
such as a behavior rewards chart, while older children
tend to respond to recognition in the form of an extra
privilege or verbal feedback such as "I am really impressed
with how hard you have been working to support your
brother's connection with mom."

• Rehearse with the child how to talk about their concerns with the resisted parent.

• Practice with the child getting and receiving feedback.

• Help the child to notice positive efforts by the resisted
parent.

• Organize with the child specific expectations for their
time with the resisted parent. For example, helping to
organize a plan of activities in collaboration with their other
parent; organizing their possessions and being ready for
the exchange on time; limiting calls or texts to the preferred
parent to once per day or genuine emergencies; respecting
their parent's household rules, routines and property; being
polite or asking for a time out if they feel emotionally out of
control. The preferred parent may want to give the child a
reward for meeting each of the expectations.

• Preferred parents usually have helpful ideas for the
resisted parent about activities the child might enjoy. For
example, the preferred parent can describe the activities,
games, TV shows and movies the child has been enjoying
in their home. The resisted parent probably would do well
to accept those kinds of ideas as peace offerings.

- The resisting child may feel inhibited about trying a new approach to their relationship with the resisted parent. The preferred parent can frame new concepts and developments for the children with metaphors or examples from other experiences. For example, "Sometimes trying a new strategy makes a big difference. Remember how hard it was to get that splinter out with your finger, but when you tried the tweezers it came right out?" Or, "Each time we get together, let's push the envelope a little towards being more polite and open about sensitive topics."

- Emphasize to the child that they need to make the best of a difficult situation. Do not suggest to the child to 'just get through' time with the other parent.

- Be clear with the child that while you love talking with them, talking with them about relationships or other problems is not a good idea when they are at that other parent's house. The preferred parent talking with the child during visits with the resisted parent often undermines the challenging, but extremely important relationship building efforts between the child and resisted parent. Furthermore, the resisted parent will feel that you are undermining their efforts to connect with the child.

Apologies by the Preferred Parent: Taking Responsibility for Their Part

Following are examples of the preferred parent (either a mom or a dad) taking responsibility for their part in the child's resistance to the other parent. Each example starts with a general statement of responsibility and then moves into specific topics related to several different family scenarios. Each example includes a response to push-back from the child, who may not want to hear that their favored parent has some responsibility for the problems with their other parent.

Mom could start with: Kids, there are some things that I need to tell you guys so that you know that I have responsibility here too and it's not just you guys and not just Dad. This is especially important to know because it really seems like you guys have pegged the situation as being all Dad's fault and none of my fault—that I am totally right in this situation and Dad is all wrong. That is simply not true, and we all have to work on this. I am at fault too. Harry, I really want you to hear this too because I am worried that you have been really focused on lashing out at Dad without end for years now, through your counseling with Dr. O, Dr. Lang, and now here. You're going over the same things over and over again, and it is time to really engage in the process of moving through and moving on. I have a part in this too, and you need to hear it so that you can really start to move past some of the history and work on a new future knowing that WE ALL contributed to how things fell apart. I'm going to name a number of specific things that I did that made things worse. You may or may not have realized them, and we are all learning. I've learned about many of them just since being here. I really, really hope that you understanding my role in the problems will help us all move forward because Dad is really genuinely accepting and working on his part too. And I don't want to hear anything about his stuff was worse than my stuff and you still don't want to work on things with him, nor do I want to hear that it's easier to forgive me because I was there more, even if I did some things wrong too. No, we all had a part to play and it is time to fix things. Period.

Scenario: *Kids being aware of Court action related to preferred parent pursuing sole custody*

Dad could say: I realize that you knowing that I was taking things to court when you guys and Mom were having a hard time wasn't helpful because you could have easily concluded I believed things weren't going to get any better with her and it would be better for you if you had less or no contact with Mom. When I told you I was taking that kind of action, you probably also thought I believed Mom's actions were bad enough for an external authority in society, the Courts, to agree Mom was bad and shouldn't have a relationship with you kids.

Kids may say: Dad, you were just trying to protect us/keep us safe/make us happy.

Dad could respond: Yes, but it is really important to understand that what I did made you feel more strongly about separating from your mother when the better thing to do was work things out and find ways to foster your relationship with Mom and to parent better with her.

Scenario: *Empowering children to decide about whether or not to have a relationship with Mother*

Dad could say: I did not do the right thing by giving you permission to decide whether or not to see your mother. I should have worked harder to direct you to mend things with her because having a positive relationship with both parents is a cornerstone of healthy development.

Kids may say: Dad, you were just listening to us and not ignoring our concerns. We are old enough to have some say in our own lives, and you recognized that.

Dad could respond: No, that's not true. I am a parent and am responsible for your behavior. I am not going to let you behave irresponsibly and engage in other detrimental behaviors. I now understand that a damaged relationship with a parent is really, really bad for people as they get older, even if things seem better in the short run. I now understand that even though it's hard to work on problems in a relationship with a parent, you need to keep working. As a parent, it is my job to take charge, just like I would if you were not doing well in school, staying out too late, breaking rules or doing anything that would put yourself in harm's way. As a parent, it's my job to protect you and make sure you stay on the right path, even if you, as the child, don't necessarily agree at any particular point in time.

Scenario: *Drove kids to resisted parent's house to collect their stuff*

Mom could say: I realize it was not healthy for me to drive you to your Dad's house to collect your belongings. By driving you there I gave you a message that I was okay with you not going over there anymore.

Kids may say: But Dad started the fighting, and he was outside with you the whole time. Dad wanted us to get our stuff out of his house as much as anybody did.

Mom could respond: This is not about Dad, as he is taking responsibility for the things he needs to. I am taking responsibility for my part. When you do the right thing, you do it because you know it. Dad may have been frustrated or angry or in his own way trying to care for you by making sure you had your stuff if you weren't going to be staying with him. I didn't know, but now I realize that MY PART was telling you by my actions that it was okay to move out from Dad's for good. It was like packing up and moving away from an old apartment or house. Because I drove you, because I allowed it, because I was a part of it, I was essentially communicating to you it was okay to cut off Dad and that I was okay with it.

Scenario: *Spoke negatively about Father in front of the kids (either directly or to others while the children were in earshot)*

Mom could say: One thing I know that was really bad was speaking negatively about your father in front of you. Regardless of my frustration or anger, I should have kept adult things between your father and me, and I should have always been supportive of your relationship with him.

Kids may say: No way, Mom. You have no idea how badly Dad spoke about you. He was always being mean about you and saying nasty things. Plus, we know that he was making things hard and wouldn't let us do our stuff. He was really nasty, and you were just being real with us.

Mom could respond: Being real would have been staying focused on the real consequences of my behaviors on you two. Real would have been realizing each of you is 50 percent me and 50 percent Dad. Talking bad about Dad is the same as me saying half of each of you is bad. That's not right, and that's not good for growing kids. People are sometimes upset and frustrated with one another, but it's not okay to dwell on it by talking negatively, especially from one parent to another. I exposed you to my negative feelings about Dad, which you both probably used as support for your feelings against Dad and you both probably used it to add fuel to the fire. Even more, I showed you a vulnerable side of me that would have allowed you both, being as sensitive as you are, to feel like for you to take care of me, your mom, you would need to attack Dad because he was the one making me feel bad. That wasn't the right thing to do. It switched roles where you were taking care of me rather than me taking care of you. Even more, it was really bad because the way you were taking care of me was thinking negatively about your father because I shared with you the negative thoughts I had about him.

Scenario: *Failure to ensure connection and engagement around special days*

Dad could say: Another thing I did not do well and that contributed to the problems was not making sure you connected with your mother on special days in a meaningful way. Holidays and special days are about the important things — close relationships with family and friends. I failed you both by not making sure that you were connecting with Mom in a better way. I really should have made sure you understood the true spirit of special days, holidays and the meaning of family.

Kids may say: Dad, seriously? She was making fun of the presents you forced us to give her and it's not like she was calling.

Dad could respond: That's not the point; you need to listen to the message I am telling you—my actions and inactions helped to create, solidify and strengthen the negative feelings you have about your mother. Had I pushed harder, like a healthy dad should have, then tension may have been lessened and maybe wouldn't have gotten to this point. By letting you guys get away with not being meaningfully engaged with Mom during things like holidays and birthdays, I was essentially telling you she is not a part of your family. Family members always connect on holiday and special days; it was wrong of me not to make it clear that you guys and she are, have always been, and will always be family. By not making it happen, I messed up really badly and made it more okay for you guys to cut her off. Cutting off a parent-child relationship is not good for you kids in the long run.

Scenario: *Not enforcing basic politeness and manners*

Mom could say: I realize now by not making sure you guys always greet your father appropriately I was unintentionally encouraging you to take away from Dad's position as your father. I was also really saying it was okay to treat him like a stranger you didn't even have to acknowledge. It was wrong and not healthy or the kind of behavior I want to role-model for you.

Kids may say: He didn't deserve to be treated nicely, and he didn't deserve to be acknowledged.

Mom could respond: No, there are basic rules about important, intimate family relationships you need to learn and respect. As your mom, it is my job to teach you how to be courteous and respectful because this is the foundation of your learning and how you will expect to treat people and be treated throughout your life. Someday you are going to have your own intimate relationships, and how you act now is likely to be similar in the future…and what you'll expect from others. I would never want you to think it is okay for your spouse or significant other to treat you without any manners even if you're fighting. To engage a family member inappropriately and without a modicum of politeness, even if there is tension, is completely unacceptable. If manners are lost, how can there be healing?

Scenario: *Inappropriately validated concerns while comforting children*

Mom could say: I now know I handled many of the situations the wrong way when you were upset about things happening with your father. By saying things like "I know," "I'm sorry about that," and "tell me about it, I lived that for ten years,"

I really made you feel as though I was agreeing your dad was a terrible, awful person who did terrible, awful things. I should have done more to make sure I was able to provide you the comfort I thought you needed, without doing more harm than good. I'm sorry.

Kids may say: Mom, we were a wreck after he came home because we were so upset after he was mean to us. You can't make him out to be a great guy if he isn't.

Mom may respond: Kids, what you have to understand is that you guys really do take a lot of direction from me, about a lot of things, even now. When you came back from Dad's upset, I should have worked harder on problem solving, either by talking with you or co-parenting with Dad to address the issues. Instead, what I did served to make you feel like Dad was a really awful guy who is incapable of change and his terrible behavior was real, the way that it has always been, was the way it would always be, and that he is incapable of change so this would be the way it would always be. That wasn't right or helpful of me.

Scenario: *Exposing children to adult-related divorce topics*

Dad could say: Adult divorce is hard enough for adults, let alone when kids get exposed to the divorce stuff. I did not know the damage I was causing when I exposed you to ideas like the Court action we talked about earlier, or even that you were supposed to be raised Catholic. It shouldn't have been anything you should have known about or had to deal with. It was for Mom and me to work those things out. We should have gotten our act together to co-parent you better, and it was wrong of me to share that information with you.

Kids may say: Well, if Mom wasn't causing problems, doing

the right thing, and following the divorce, then it wouldn't even have been an issue.

Dad could respond: I now know that by sharing that type of information, I was essentially telling you Mom can't be trusted, doesn't follow the rules, and she is making our lives difficult. That was a harmful and destructive message to give you; it made things worse between you guys and your mom. I should have kept adult stuff as adult stuff and kid stuff as kid stuff. I do not share information with you about my taxes or my retirement savings because it is adult stuff, and not things for you to have to deal with. In the same way, I should not have shared divorce-related information with you.

Understanding the Co-Parenting Trap

OVER THE TWO TO THREE YEARS following separation and divorce, most parents[8] experience a reduction in anger and hostile behaviors as they disengage emotionally from their former partners and move ahead with their separate lives. *Cooperative co-parenting*, is achieved by 25 to 30 percent of divorced parents. The majority of parents—more than half—settle into *parallel co-parenting* in which emotional disengagement from each other, low conflict, and low communication predominate.

Between 20 to 25 percent of parents have a *high-conflict co-parenting* relationship characterized by poor communication, low cooperation, high distrust, and failed decision-making. Sometimes conflicted co-parenting results in what psychologists call an "Intractable Conflict"[9] or "conflict traps";[10] these are

---

8. Kelly, J. B. (2012). Risk and Protective Factors Associated with Child and Adolescent Adjustment following Separation and Divorce: Social Science Applications. In Kuehnle, K. & Drozd, L. (Eds.) *Parenting Plan Evaluation: Applied Research for the Family Court*. New York: Oxford University Press. 63-64.

situations when people's reactions to the conflict make the conflict worse.

In the co-parenting trap, the co-parents' responses to parenting challenges lead them into entrenched beliefs that their co-parent lacks critical parenting skills. It is important to understand that the co-parenting trap exerts powerful psychological forces on parents which shape how they think, feel and react. A parent caught in the co-parenting trap may believe their thoughts, feelings and actions are reasonable; in fact, they tend to feel highly confident they are right. But the co-parenting trap draws out the worst in everyone in the family. Parents who are usually calm, loving and level headed are triggered again and again into anger, disgust and righteousness, and they are strongly tempted to make hostile comments and view their co-parent as defective, perhaps even seriously disturbed; a parent without any redeeming qualities.

Two patterns characteristic of people stuck in a conflict[11] such as the co-parenting trap are: 1) they tend to deny or discount any and all positive information about the opposing person; and 2) they feel overwhelmingly resistant to act differently toward the opposing person whom they view as causing misery to them. As Peter Coleman wrote:

"For a person in the throes of a powerful, long-term conflict,

---

9. Some people dislike the term "Intractable" as they see it as too negative: Intractable conflicts are impossible to resolve, they say, so people think they are not worth dealing with. Nevertheless, there is a set of conflicts out there that are hard to deal with: "Protracted." "Destructive." "Deep-rooted." "Resolution-resistant." "Intransigent." "Gridlocked." "Identity-based." "Needs based." "Complex." "Difficult." "Malignant." and "Chronic High-Conflict Divorces". See: http://www.beyondintractability.org/essay/meaning-intractability.
10. Coleman, P.T. (2011). *The Five Percent: Finding Solutions to (Seemingly) Impossible Conflicts.* New York: Public Affairs, Perseus Books.
11. *Ibid.*

misperception and misunderstanding rule. Concerns over obtaining accurate information [are replaced by] defending our sense of the Truth and what is Right. These may of course be valid concerns.

But when everything makes perfect sense in a complicated conflict, when who the good guys and the bad guys are is perfectly clear, we must be all the more vigilant [about the tendency toward biased thinking]."

The intractable conflict[12] of the co-parenting trap is like a black hole that draws-in and extinguishes the light of family love that children require. It is as if the divorce trap attracts negative family interaction and repulses positive family interactions. For example, if either parent does something intended to reduce the conflict, the behavior's benign intention may disappear and be misinterpreted as a manipulation, or an insincere and short-lived gesture. Years of effort to be a good parent and partner disappear, and are replaced solely with dramatic anecdotes of personality and parenting incompetence.

How Intractable Conflict Escalates: A Five-Phase Model[13]

Stage 1: Normal Everyday Conflict. Even good relationships have moments of conflict. These can be resolved with care and mutual empathy. In this stage, people look for cooperative solutions. If a solution is not found, especially because one of the parties stubbornly sticks to his or her point of view, the conflict escalates.

---

12. Vallacher, R.R., et al. (2010). Rethinking Intractable Conflict: The Perspective of Dynamical Systems. *American Psychologist*, 65(4), 262-278.

13. Douglas E. Noll, Esq. is a lawyer and mediator specializing in difficult and intractable conflicts. Mr. Noll holds a Master's Degree in Peacemaking and Conflict Studies. Mr. Noll is a Fellow of the International Academy of Mediators, a Fellow of the American College of Civil Trial Mediators, and serves on numerous national arbitration panels. Website: www.nollassociates.com

Stage 2: Fluctuation between Cooperation and Competition. Information is exchanged, but as tension mounts, arguments in favor of one's own position are presented more forcefully, often over and over. Increasingly less effort is made to empathize with, and express respect for the concerns of the co-parent. Convincing or winning over the opposing side with logic becomes the goal, rather than to clarify misunderstandings and miscommunications.

Stage 3: Concrete Actions. The parents each lose hope for a reasonable outcome. Attorneys are retained and winning becomes the goal. Interaction becomes hostile. Stereotyping is applied negatively to the opposing parent.

Stage 4: Cognitive Functioning Regresses. One believes they are aware of the other's perspectives, but defensiveness and planning counter-arguments replace deep listening and exploration of the co-parent's thoughts, feelings or interpretation of the situation.

Stage 5: Comprehensive Ideology and Totalizing of Antagonistic Perspectives. Sacred values, convictions and superior moral obligations are at stake. The conflict touches the deepest parts of each person's belief system and is tied into relationships with friends and family. By threatening and creating fear, both parties strive toward total control of the situation, leaving no room for compromise, thereby escalating conflict further.

Why Co-Parenting Traps Persist[14]

A defining feature of parents and children caught in the co-parenting trap is their tendency to resist discussion of their

---

14. Pruitt, Dean G. and Rubin, Jeffrey Z. (1986). *Social Conflict: Escalation, Stalemate and Settlement.* New York: Random House.

beliefs and attitudes about the co-parent. It is like trying to talk about politics or religion – it's easier to talk with others with similar attitudes, and sometimes very difficult to hear out those with opposing beliefs.

Negative attitudes toward the other parent tend to be maintained by four primary psychological mechanisms: *selective perception, self-fulfilling prophecy, passive-aggressive hostility* and *stereotyping.*

Selective Perception is using a personal filter for what we see and hear to ensure they suit our own needs. Selective perception leads us to pay attention to information that supports our existing attitudes, and to ignore or discount information that challenges what we believe. Selective perception tends to operate unconsciously.

Self-fulfilling Prophecies arise when a parent's expectations about their co-parent cause them to act in ways that actually provoke the expected response from the co-parent. For example, a co-parent does not return communications promptly because they expect hostility; then when the co-parent insists on a timely response, they view him/her as angry, controlling and aggressive.

Passive Aggressive Hostility describes how co-parents tend to reduce or break off communication when they encounter conflict with their co-parent. When too little information is exchanged, misunderstandings develop without a communication channel available to correct misinformation or misunderstandings. Passive aggressive hostility means that co-parents stay stuck in the belief that their co-parent is not to be trusted and the belief that co-parenting cooperation is impossible. When a co-parent selectively attends to information critical of the co-parent, and seals themselves off from information which might contradict their negative views of the co-parent, the trap is set.

Stereotyping provides an oversimplified explanation for the cause of the conflict and is used to justify co-parenting non-cooperation. For example, a parent might say, "Jeff does not see his children as being more important than other things. The girls rank far below his true priorities—himself, his girlfriend, his girlfriend's daughters, his work, his money [...] His narcissistic personality disorder leads him to believe that he can fool and convince anyone of anything. He clearly intends to continue using our children to hurt me, and I will always do all I can to protect them."

Overcoming the Co-Parenting Trap

Stalemates

At the point of stalemate, neither parent wishes to escalate the conflict further, though neither is yet able or willing to take the actions to consistently be able to arrive at co-parenting agreements about the children. Stalemates happen when the parents exhaust their resources and the costs of continued overt conflict have become unacceptable. Stalemates represent a balance of effective power: neither side has the power to move the other.

Co-parenting stalemates can be broken by yielding, withdrawing or by the co-parents successfully negotiating parenting agreements. Usually both parents feel that they have done more than enough yielding to the other parent. Typically, the preferred parent is accused of withdrawing their support for the relationship between the child and the resisted parent, and of acting as though the children's loss of relationship with the resisted parent is sad, but necessary. The last option for most resisted parents is to withdraw their efforts to salvage the relationship with their child. Hopefully, the parents resolve the

---

15. Coleman, P.T. (2011). *The Five Percent: Finding Solutions to (Seemingly) Impossible Conflicts.* New York: Public Affairs, Perseus Books, 106-107.

stalemate through renewed efforts to negotiate co-parenting agreements.

Negotiating Co-Parenting Agreements

Skillfully helping a child who is resisting a parent requires that the co-parents negotiate what can loom as an apparently endless series of issues and situations. Negotiating and problem-solving through intractable conflict is,[15] "A slow, gradual process of disentangling fears, assumptions and misinformation from facts on the ground. [It is] a *highly emotional* set of encounters involving two processes: breaking down negative assumptions, beliefs, and feelings regarding the 'other' and *building-up* new constructive, compassionate, cooperative relationships [...]."

Co-parents and children successfully coping with the anger and resentment they feel towards one another makes-or-breaks the journey out of the co-parenting trap. Since we think in terms of cause and effect, the first urge is to figure out who did what wrong so that they can recognize the error of their ways, apologize for their mistake(s), and offer a pledge to do better in the future. Seems reasonable. Sounds good. Doesn't work.

There are lots of reasons that talking about the past to isolate root causes does not work. Most behavior is too complicated to identify simple causes. Family members usually have different memories of what happened. And, family members interpret differently what motivated the behavior or the justification for it.

To assist a child overcome the barriers they have towards a parent, co-parents are faced with the considerable challenge of mounting a new platform for communication when the history of hurts, resentments, and past co-parenting failures can be summoned in a micro-second with a careless word or expression. Mention of ugly past family events usually gets everyone defensive before the opening statement has been completed – broaching the topic sounds the alarm to 'man your battle stations.' As an example of such an exchange: one parent says, "I have been very upset since last weekend when you pushed me." The other parent counters : "You are leaving out the part about how you got up in my face and I asked you to stop and move back before I tried to move you away from me." The single most important reason for seeking the assistance of a behavioral health professional is to help the family conversation to stay out of the past and focused on what needs to happen next. It is extremely difficult for family members to let go of the desire to remedy a past injustice by placing blame, clarifying the nature and extent of their hurt feelings, and asking for validation that their grievance is justified.

When a child is resisting a parent, co-parenting communication nearly always requires the assistance of a forensically informed behavioral health professional who has experience with families caught in the co-parenting trap, to guide the co-parents' efforts at communication. Inexperienced professionals may inadvertently aggravate the co-parenting trap by becoming aligned with one parent's perspective, undermining the power of their neutral role and losing the trust of the other parent.

There are multiple advantages to using the services of a behavioral health professional:

1. The professional's office provides the parents a neutral and safe setting for talking. The professional acts as a referee, a conversation manager, ensuring that co-parenting dialogue is polite, respectful, and solution-focused rather than blame-focused.

2. The professional helps the parents to identify their concerns and interests; set the order of issues to be addressed; establish timelines and deadlines for action; and bring to bear

public pressure and accountability.

3. By offering their professional views and experiences with problems the parents are encountering, they can help the parents develop a more informed understanding of the issues, and what needs to be done to address them. The professional keeps the conversation on topic to agenda rather than jumping from one problem to the next, or from the present and future to the past.

4. The professional assists the parents to maintain their emotional composure by expressing compassion for the turmoil encountered in the divorce trap; recognizing the efforts the parents are making individually and collectively; encouraging the parents to stay true to co-parenting goals and ties; and encouraging the parents to make concessions and be flexible rather than rigid and defensive in their approach to co-parenting.

Parenting Tips for Negotiating Co-Parenting Agreements

- Set an agenda: Avoid surprises; agree with ex on the agenda in advance to help you stay on track instead of veering off into emotionally charged tangents.

- Begin the conversation: Start with an affirmation of commitment to being amicable; develop ground rules for each partner's response to get the conversation back on track if it becomes heated.

- Seek to understand: Use Active Listening skills. When we feel that we are being attacked, we tend to plan a response to what is being said rather than trying to get clarification of what is being said. An important step in managing a delicate co-parenting conversation is to demonstrate that you are listening carefully and trying to understand completely and clearly what is being said. Promote active listening by paraphrasing or repeating what you heard the other say, not your interpretation of it, or ask a question to clarify your understanding. Make sure the other person believes your understanding is accurate. Get more details as to when, how and under what circumstances the problem exists.

• Focus on the future rather than analyzing the past: Bill Eddy, LCSW, Esq[16] shows how making proposals avoids talking about past problems in favor of a solution-focused future. For example, "You spend too much time making a fuss at exchanges, no wonder Tiffany doesn't want to come with me," becomes, "How about if we agree that you will say goodbye to Tiffany in private before you arrive at the exchange, and I will do the same on my end."

• Avoid lecturing: As much as you feel you are right and have something to say and a right to say it, the truth is, the more drawn out you are, the more you lose your effectiveness. The more briefly you make your point the better. We tend to lecture when we are not sure we can make a point without providing a lot of justification for our position. We go on and on about all the reasons we feel we are right.

• Respond to attacks and criticism: Concentrate on listening; acknowledge the concern (which curbs the energy of the attack or criticism). Look for the concern underlying the attack; try to restate the concern neutrally; ask for clarification about what the other wants.

• Express criticism: Introduce the fact that you have a criticism or problem you would like to discuss before you state what the complaint is. Admit these kinds of discussions haven't gone well in the past and that you don't want the co-parent to feel defensive. When you bring up your concern, describe the problem rather than character-izing your spouse's behavior; do not attribute motives, intention or fault to them.

Neutral phrases to defuse a fight that is going nowhere:

- "We see it differently; our perceptions are different, so let's just move on."
- "We have different needs in this situation."
- "Can we agree to disagree?"
- "This is not working for me."
- "There is no point in arguing over who is right. Can we look for a way to handle this from this point forward?"
- "This discussion is not productive. It is hurtful."
- "What we are doing now is not helpful; let's stop."

The Path for Overcoming the Co-Parenting Trap

It is difficult to predict how a family will work its way out of the co-parenting trap. Some co-parents are ready to re-organize how they interact with one another, and redefine what behaviors they expect from the children towards the co-parent. In those families, change can be rapid. Some co-parents continue with strong resistance towards one another, but are willing to adopt and consistently implement agreements negotiated with the assistance of a third party. In those families, agreements lead away from conflict and towards restored family

---

16. Eddy, B. (2014) *So What's Your Proposal; Shifting high-Conflict People From Blaming to Problem-solving in 30 Seconds!* Scottsdale, AZ: Unhooked Books.

relationships, but progress tends to be gradual, and marked by occasional eruptions of family conflict. In some families the co-parents and the children need a lot of support and treatment to put aside their animosity towards one another and to find respectful communication and interaction patterns. Tragically, in some families the anger and resentment will not abate, and the children grow up displaced from a parent and parts of their extended family.

Though there are differences in how families travel the path through the co-parenting trap, in each instance it requires a coordinated effort among the parents along with their new partners; the children and stepchildren; and third parties like the court, attorneys and behavioral health professionals. Intractable conflict such as found in the co-parenting trap is not isolated to families. Here is a description by Mari Fitzduff, Director of the Conflict and Coexistence Programme at Brandeis University, of how the lengthy conflict in Northern Ireland gave way to resolution:

"Then all the dominoes began to fall and it was fairly clear that peace was coming, albeit fairly slowly, to Northern Ireland. But it always does come like this, and I always say conflicts end not with a bang but a whimper after whimper after whimper.

I think the best knowledge you have is peace is really just like a jigsaw, and there's different times when you can do different things. So some days all you can do is pick up the bodies, comfort the wounded, and try to make sure it doesn't spiral into violence. Other days you look up and you realize, God, we've got time to think about integrated education. There's what I call short term, medium, and long term, and you really need to have people working on them all. So in a way it's taking advantage of all of the different opportunities that you get within a conflict, given that there often are times when some days are not as bad as others and some years might not be as bad as others."

Perhaps the greatest challenge to emerging from the co-parenting trap, is taking positive steps towards family unity when given the history of hurts which lead the family into the trap. In his poem "If", Rudyard Kipling describes the kind of focus required from parents and children to overcome the negative emotions and family dynamics of the co-parenting trap:

> If you can keep your head when all about you
> Are losing theirs and blaming it on you,
> If you can trust yourself when all men doubt you,
> But make allowance for their doubting too;
> If you can wait and not be tired by waiting,
> Or being lied about, don't deal in lies,
> Or being hated, don't give way to hating,
> And yet don't look too good, nor talk too wise [...]
> If you can bear to hear the truth you've spoken
> Twisted by knaves to make a trap for fools,
> Or watch the things you gave your life to, broken,
> And stoop and build 'em up with worn-out tools:
> If you can make one heap of all your winnings
> And risk it on one turn of pitch-and-toss,
> And lose, and start again at your beginnings
> And never breathe a word about your loss;
> If you can force your heart and nerve and sinew
> To serve your turn long after they are gone,
> And so hold on when there is nothing in you
> Except the Will which says to them: 'Hold on!

If co-parents can muster that level of focus and resolve, they will be able to negotiate the path out of the co-parenting trap.

Anger, Resentment and Forgiveness

FORGIVENESS IS A UNIVERSALLY recognized approach for reducing the anger and resentment[17] over past events. The importance of forgiveness is a central belief of most religious and spiritual traditions, but family members caught in the co-parent trap can have sharp reservations about the idea of forgiving one another. It is hard to imagine a parent wanting for themselves or their child to be burdened with abiding anger. But if a counselor suggests forgiving the other parent, or the child forgiving the parent, the counselor might quickly be viewed as biased toward the parent who needs to be forgiven, or not understanding how deep the hurt was, or how bad the offending parent is. The first order of business when thinking about forgiveness is to get clear about what it is and what it is not.

---

17. Robert C. Solomon, a professor of philosophy at the University of Texas at Austin, says resentment, contempt and anger are similar but different. Resentment is directed toward higher-status individuals, anger is directed toward equal-status individuals, and contempt is directed toward lower-status individuals. Co-parents are angry with one another, and the child has resentment toward the resisted parent. For our purpose, anger and resentment are talked about interchangeably.

Let's start with what forgiveness is *not*:

- Forgiveness is not condoning, excusing or putting up with offending behavior.
- Forgiveness is not self-disempowerment.
- Forgiveness is not giving up the healing power of anger.
- Forgiveness is not committing to re-storing the prior relationship, although it implies an initiative towards more harmonious interactions.
- Forgiveness is not forgetting the offense.
- Forgiveness is not letting time heal the wounds.
- Forgiveness is not balancing the scales, for example, "I will forgive you if you will apologize."
- Forgiveness is not a quick fix.
- Forgiveness is not revenge-based, for example, accepting what happened knowing that God will punish the person.
- Forgiveness is not a single decision or one-time event.
- Forgiveness is not a blind decision to trust again.

A person can decide to forgive and then change their mind.

What Forgiveness Is

A commonly held view[18] is that forgiveness is a choice by a betrayed person to shift their own *internal response* to the offending person away from bitterness and angry thoughts towards peace and compassion. For example, a woman betrayed by her former spouse said "I released him to God." However, the decision to forgive does not mark the end of angry thoughts and feelings. Forgiveness means working on old wounds and memories and

---

18. Legaree, T., Turner, J. and Lollis, S. (2007). Forgiveness and Therapy: A Critical Review of Conceptualizations, Practices and Values Found in the Literature. *Journal of Marital and Family Therapy*, 33(2), 192-213.

associated feelings until they diminish over time.

The purpose of forgiveness is to do good; to be a moral person. A person who forgives has been treated unjustly. "Forgiveness is a merciful response to the injustice. The one who forgives has a clear sense of right and wrong, concludes that the other acted wrongly, and offers mercy."[19] When a person is merciful, they offer the offending person good things that are not deserved and the forgiving person refrains from a punishing attitude that may be deserved.

In the context of a separated family, forgiveness is also the first step to healing. But can one make the decision to forgive without feeling emotionally ready to do so? Sometimes this is the only choice. Family feuds can go on for a long time. Children typically use denial as a first line of defense against their hurt feelings, and may earnestly believe that loss of relationship with a parent is no big deal. Parents may have to require that the child keep talking about the dispute when they prefer not to, and to think and talk in a real way about what is going on from everyone's point of view, not only their own.

Conclusion

There are few passions in life stronger than a parent's love. When a parent feels their child's well-being is threatened, or when a parent feels the bond with their child is threatened, the deepest and strongest emotions engage. Parents working to restore family unity and a child's relationship with a resisted parent are under severe stress. They need realistic expectations about how difficult the challenge is and what is required to

---

19. Enright, R.D. & Fitzgibbons, R.P. (2000). *Helping Clients Forgive: An Empirical Guide for Resolving Anger and Restoring Hope.* Washington, D.C.: American Psychological Association, 23.

resolve it. They need special skills to respond to the unique family challenges which occur when a child resists a parent. They need lots of support from one another, friends, and family members. And they need unshakable resolve to maintain emotional composure and exercise their best parenting skills.

Divorce & Co-Parenting Resources

Children of Divorce – Coping with Divorce: Online program for kids with divorcing parents, developed at ASU by Dr. Jessie Boring and Irwin Sandler to reduce mental health problems and increase coping efficacy. http://familytransitions-ptw. com/CoDCoD/parents/index.html

---

Our Family Wizard – electronic communication for co-parents. http://ourfamilywizard.com/ofw/

Arizona Supreme Court (2009). Planning for Parenting Time/ Arizona's Guide for Parents Living Apart. Currently linked at: http://www.azcourts.gov/portals/31/parentingtime/ ppwguidelines.pdf

---

Arizona AFCC (2011) Co-Parenting Communication Guide Currently linked at: http://azafcc.org/resources/

Office of the Attorney General, Texas (2008). For Our Children – Learning to Work Together: Co-parenting Guide. Currently linked at: https://www.texasattorneygeneral.gov/ ag_publications/pdfs/coparenting.pdf

New Ways for Families: Online parenting class for high-conflict cases: https://newways4families.onlineparentingprograms.com/

ProperComm: website providing resources and direct support for parents to make their electronic communication appropriate, eliminating hostility and emotion. https://www.propercomm.com/

Welcome Back, Pluto: Understanding, Preventing and Overcoming Parental Alienation (DVD) By Dr. Richard Warshak. For purchase at: http://www.warshak.com/

Eddy, Bill, LCSW, Esq. (2010). *Don't Alienate the Kids.* HCI Press. For purchase at: http://www.unhookedbooks.com/

Farber, Edward, Ph.D (2013). *Raising the Kid You Love with the Ex You Hate.* Greenleaf Book Group Press. For purchase at: http://www.amazon.com/

Thayer, Elizabeth and Zimmerman, Jeffrey (2001). *Co-Parenting Survival Guide.* New Harbinger. For purchase at: http://www.amazon.com/

Stahl, Philip, Ph.D (2007). *Parenting After Divorce: Resolving Conflicts and Meeting your Children's Needs.* Rebuilding Books. For purchase at: http://parentingafterdivorce.com/books/

Carter, Debra (2015). *CoParenting After Divorce: A GPS For Raising Healthy Kids.* Unhooked Books. Release date April 2015

Unhooked Books: Online divorce & co-parenting bookstore. http://www.unhookedbooks.com/

Notes

Notes

Notes

Made in the
USA
Columbia, SC